YOUR MINDSET IS YOUR ASSET

IT WILL SHAPE YOUR DESTINY

KRUNAL PRAJAPATI
DHRUVIL PATEL

Contents

Preface   *v*

Acknowledgements   *vii*

  1. What Is Mindset?   1

  2. Time Is The Most Valuable Asset   6

  3. THE GREAT MINDSET AND GREAT TIME   22
     ALWAYS PAYS OFF.

  4. Worrier Vs Warrior Mentality   48

Final Words on "Your Mindset is Your Asset"   63

A Note on the author   65

A Note on the co-author   67

Reach Out   69

PREFACE

Writing this book has been a journey of self-discovery and empowerment. It all started with a conversation with one of my closest friends and the positive thoughts that have guided me through my own struggles. Those moments of shared reflection sparked something deep within me—the desire to write down my experiences and insights on mindset, to help others who might be going through similar challenges.

Mindset has played a crucial role in my life. It has been the driving force behind overcoming obstacles and the foundation of any success I've achieved. As I reflect on my personal journey of growth, I realize how much my own mindset evolved over time. Writing this book became not just a way to share knowledge, but an opportunity for self-introspection. It allowed me to gain clarity on my goals and strengthen my determination to pursue them.

This book is not just a guide—it's a tool to empower you. I want you to walk away from these pages feeling inspired, capable, and ready to take action. The purpose of Your Mindset Is Your Asset is to show you that you have the ability to transform your life by changing the way you think. If you're ready to embrace that transformation, then this book is for you.

The idea for this book came from a moment of realization, sparked by the people and experiences that inspired me along the way. It took me about a year to write, a year filled with balancing work, family, and writing. There were moments when it felt overwhelming, but I found that the best way to move forward was to take breaks, gain inspiration from other books, and trust the process.

One of the reasons I wrote this book was to offer something fresh. While many books discuss the concept of mindset, they often rely on outdated information. This book is different. It offers practical insights that are relevant to the world we live in today. And I believe it's more important than ever to understand the power of your mindset in navigating the complexities of modern life.

You might be wondering, "Who is this book for?" The truth is, this book is for anyone who wants to improve their life by strengthening their mindset. There is no one specific "ideal reader," because the message I share is universal. Whether you're struggling with doubt or simply seeking growth, the principles in this book can help you overcome obstacles and find the strength to reach your goals.

If there's one piece of advice I can offer as you begin this journey, it's this: believe in yourself, trust the process, and know that the power to change is already within you. The lessons in this book are meant to guide you, to support you, and to remind you that you have the strength to overcome anything life throws your way.

The core message of this book is simple yet powerful: Nobody cares about you, except you. So, believe in yourself and in God, and you will overcome anything.

Thank you for taking the time to read Your Mindset Is Your Asset. I hope these pages inspire you to believe in your power to change and take control of your future.

ACKNOWLEDGEMENTS

First and foremost, I would like to extend my deepest gratitude to my dear friend and coauthor, Dhruvil Patel. Your unwavering support, insightful feedback, and tireless dedication have been invaluable throughout this journey. From the early brainstorming sessions to the final stages of writing and editing, your contributions were essential to bringing this book to life.

A special thanks also goes to Dhruvil for being my pillar of support during the toughest moments. Your encouragement and belief in this project kept me going when the path was uncertain.

I would also like to acknowledge Andrew Tate for his inspiring thoughts and wisdom, which helped shape the content and direction of this book.

Lastly, to all the readers who believed in this journey and supported the idea of Your Mindset Is Your Asset, thank you for your trust and enthusiasm. This book exists because of your belief in its message.

I

What Is Mindset?

Mindset is the foundation of who we are and what we can achieve. It's a unique thought process—a perspective that cannot be borrowed, bought, or inherited from others. It is something we create within ourselves, shaped by our beliefs, experiences, and determination to achieve something meaningful. But

what makes mindset so powerful?

It's the strength behind every goal we set and every path we choose to walk. When you are truly committed to your dreams, the first transformation happens in your mind. You prepare yourself, mentally and emotionally, to face the journey ahead. It's this preparation—this mindset—that fuels your capability, strengthens your faith, and ignites your willingness to achieve what may seem impossible. As they say, **"The mindset of a person is their way of living."**

It's not just about thinking positively; it's about cultivating a mental framework that aligns with your goals, your values, and your vision for the future.

Sir Ratan Tata, one of India's most respected business leaders, once said, ***"Take a decision, work upon it, and make it right."*** These words encapsulate the essence of a powerful mindset. It's not about waiting for the perfect moment or the perfect plan; it's about trusting yourself to take action and adjust along the way.

The Power of Mindset: A Story of Conor McGregor

Let's delve into a real-life example that illustrates the transformative power of mindset—Conor McGregor, the Irish mixed martial artist who rose from humble beginnings to global stardom.

McGregor's journey wasn't paved with comfort or privilege. Before he became a UFC champion, he worked as a plumber, spending his days in the monotony of a trade that didn't align with his dreams. But deep down, he had a vision—a burning desire to achieve greatness. He decided that his life was meant for something extraordinary, and he began to work tirelessly towards his goal of becoming the best in the world of mixed martial arts.

McGregor once said, ***"Believe in yourself. Manifest yourself. Because manifesting ourselves is the greatest process of becoming the person we are meant to be."***

Armed with this belief, he didn't just dream; he took relentless action. He immersed himself in training, pushed through countless hardships, and faced adversities with unshakable determination. His journey wasn't easy, but his mindset kept him focused. And eventually, his efforts paid off—he became the featherweight UFC champion, one of the richest and most celebrated fighters in the sport's history.

McGregor's words resonate with anyone chasing a dream: ***"Provide some amount of time to yourself. Work upon your goals. Be different from others."***

This isn't just advice; it's a way of life. To achieve greatness, you must dedicate time and effort to nurturing your vision, crafting strategies, and staying committed even when the road gets tough.

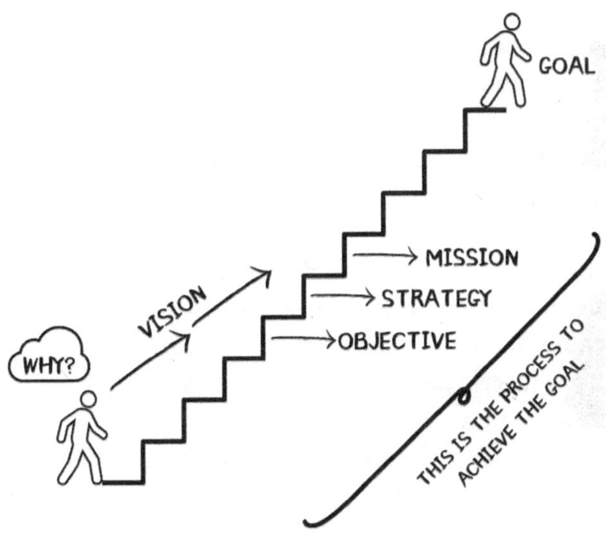

Your "Why" Is the Key

A person armed with a vision, an idea, and a purpose can achieve anything. Why? Because clarity in their "why" fuels their journey. When you truly understand what you want to do and why it matters, every challenge becomes surmountable. The fog clears, and the path forward reveals itself.

As McGregor once said, *"When you see into your mind and have the courage to speak it out, it will definitely happen."*

This courage—to believe in your dreams, to declare them, and to act upon them—is the cornerstone of a winning mindset.

Building Your Mindset

Take a moment to reflect: What is your goal? What is your vision? Do you have the strength to pursue it? Your mindset is the foundation that determines how far you'll go. It is not just about talent or resources; it's about the mental strength to stay focused, resilient, and determined.

Every great achievement starts with a decision—a decision to believe in yourself and commit to the process. As you embark on your journey, remember the stories of those who came before you, like Conor McGregor, who proved that no matter where you start, it's your mindset that determines where you end up.

Let this chapter inspire you to nurture a mindset that will serve as your compass, guiding you toward the life you've always envisioned.

Key Points

1. **What is Mindset?** Mindset is a personal framework shaped by determination and self-belief.
2. **Commitment Drives Success:** A strong mindset prepares you to face challenges and pursue goals with resilience.
3. **Lessons from Conor McGregor:** Believe in yourself, manifest your goals, and work relentlessly to achieve them.
4. **Clarity is Key:** Knowing your "why" gives purpose and direction to your efforts.
5. **Key Takeaway:** A winning mindset is the foundation for overcoming obstacles and achieving greatness.

II

Time Is the Most Valuable Asset

Time is often referred to as our best friend. It's the one companion that never leaves us, the silent force that propels us forward—or holds us back—depending on how we choose to spend it. Time is a resource like no other. It's the one thing we can never get back once it's gone, and yet, so often, we take it for granted.

Time Respects Those Who Respect It

Just as a loyal friend will stand by you when you honor and nurture the relationship, time, too, respects those who make the most of it. When you value time, when you invest it wisely, it multiplies in ways that bring you closer to your goals, deeper into your growth, and more fulfilled in your journey.

But here's the truth: Time doesn't wait for anyone. It moves forward, whether we're ready or not. The question is: are you making the most of it? Are you respecting time, or are you letting it slip through your fingers?

Opportunities and the Role of Time

In our lives, God—or the universe, depending on your beliefs—gives us countless opportunities. These moments are like windows opening to new possibilities, offering us chances to change, to grow, to improve. But just like time itself, opportunities don't last forever. They come, and if we don't recognize them, they fade away.

Unfortunately, many people fail to see these opportunities or take them for granted. We hesitate, we doubt, and sometimes we let fear prevent us from stepping through those doors of possibility. We fail to take action, and before we know it, that opportunity is gone. In those moments, the regret can be crippling.

However, it's not about how many times we miss those opportunities—it's about how we respond when we do. The greatest minds throughout history have said that failure isn't the end; it's part of the process. As one wise person once said, ***"Failure is the best medicine to cure success."***

This powerful statement reminds us that failure is not a punishment; it's a lesson. Every failed attempt is an opportunity to learn, to adapt, and to grow. The greatest achievements often come after the deepest failures. The key is not to give up when things get hard but to see failure as a stepping stone on the path to success.

Turning Failure Into Fuel

Failure can sting, there's no doubt about it. It can be painful, discouraging, and make us question everything. But if we allow it to, failure becomes one of the most powerful catalysts for success. It's through failure that we build resilience, sharpen our skills, and develop the wisdom that allows us to thrive.

Think of the most successful people in the world. They didn't reach the top without facing adversity. They failed—repeatedly. But what set them apart was their refusal to stay down. They took each failure as an opportunity to grow stronger, more determined, and more capable.

So, if you face a setback, remember this: it's not the end. It's just another lesson, another step forward. Don't fear failure—embrace it. And never let time slip away while you're sitting on the sidelines, waiting for the perfect moment. The best time to start is always now.

The Power of Now

Time is a gift that only the present moment can offer. Yesterday is gone, and tomorrow is uncertain. All we truly have is the here and now. Don't let the fear of failure or the anxiety of the unknown hold you back from making the most of this precious resource.

This chapter is a call to action. A reminder to respect time, to value the opportunities you've been given, and to take bold action toward your dreams. Time waits for no one, so don't wait for the perfect moment. Start now. You have everything you need to create the life you've always wanted—if you're willing to invest your time wisely and embrace every opportunity that comes your way.

STORY ABOUT AN ANT.

This story may seem familiar, but it's one we need to revisit often. Why? Because it serves as a powerful reminder of perseverance and the importance of never giving up, no matter how tough the journey.

Imagine an ant, small and determined, climbing a tree. It's not easy, and she struggles to reach her goal. Again and again, she tries, pushing herself despite the obstacles in her path. Each time she falters, she picks herself up and continues, not stopping until she finally reaches her destination.

This story is a beautiful example of tenacity. The ant doesn't give up because she knows that success requires persistence. If she had stopped, she would never have reached her goal. The lesson here is simple: to achieve your dreams, you must keep pushing forward, no matter how many times you fall or fail.

We often hear people talk about wanting success, but the truth is, many aren't willing to put in the work. They want things to come easily, without struggle or effort. But success doesn't work that way. Not even the universe or God can give you what you want if you aren't willing to work for it.

Time: Your Best and Worst Friend

Time is a powerful force. It can be your greatest ally, or it can slip away from you, leaving you with regrets. The difference lies in how you respect it. When you honor time—when you use it wisely—it rewards you. But if you waste it, it becomes your worst enemy.

Think of it as a relationship: respect time, and it will respect you. Don't take it for granted, don't squander it, and don't delay your actions. Time is precious, and it will either help you achieve your dreams or leave you behind.

Manifestation and the Power of Action

When you truly believe in yourself, when you commit to your dreams with unwavering faith, things begin to happen. You manifest your desires into reality. But remember, manifestation isn't just about thinking positively. It's about action. It's about putting in the effort, staying committed, and believing that the universe will align with your hard work.

Greatness is not achieved by everyone. It's earned by those who understand the power of mindset and action. It's those who are willing to do what it takes, to keep going when others quit, and to pursue their vision with relentless determination.

THE GREAT MINDSET IS ACHIEVED ONLY BY FEW,

NOT BY EVERYONE.

THE WISE ONE

AMONG THE FOOLS A WISE ONE

WILL ALWAYS BE WRONG

The Matrix of Society

Let's talk about the world we live in. We often hear about "the matrix"—a metaphor for the system in which society operates, shaped by collective beliefs, expectations, and norms. The majority of people follow the same path, the same mindset, driven by the same external influences. They conform to what society expects from them, limiting their own potential.

But then, there are the outliers—the ones who think differently, the ones who choose to break free from the matrix. These are the few who decide to follow their own path, to think outside the box, and to challenge the status quo. These are the visionaries, the dreamers, the ones who carve out new possibilities.

In today's world, it's so easy to get caught up in what everyone else is doing. We live in an era of influence—where social media, trends, and the opinions of others shape our choices. But here's the truth: when you let society dictate your every move, you lose sight of who you really are. You become so focused on following the crowd that you forget to listen to your own voice.

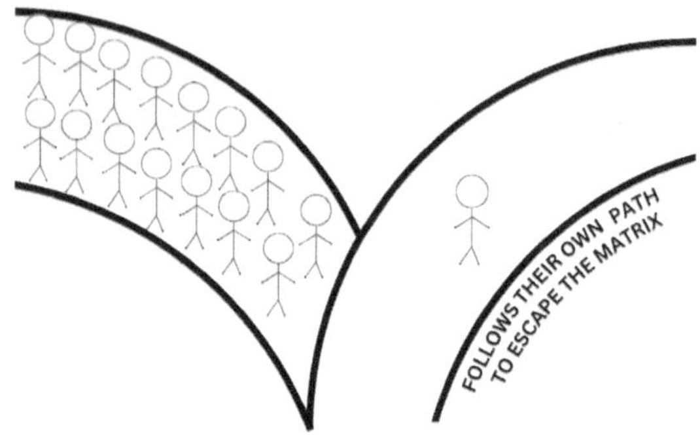

Breaking Free from Society's Expectations

A person with a great mindset understands the importance of following their own path, regardless of societal pressure. They aren't afraid to stand out or to live differently. They know that true fulfillment comes from living in alignment with their dreams, not from conforming to the expectations of others.

Unfortunately, many people allow societal pressures to hold them back. They fear judgment, they fear rejection, and so they follow the crowd. They let the world tell them who they should be, what they should want, and how they should live. But the truly great people in this world are the ones who've chosen to *illuminate their own mindset*. They're the ones who've embraced their individuality and gone after what they truly want, not what society says they should want.

Illuminating Your Mindset: The Path to Greatness

As one great thinker said, **"Illumination of the mindset is the great process to achieve great."** What does this mean? It means that your mindset is your guiding light. The more you refine and illuminate it, the more clarity you will gain about your purpose, your vision, and your path.

Start by embracing your own uniqueness. Stop trying to fit into a mold that was created by others. The moment you begin to see yourself as capable of greatness, you begin to align your actions with your dreams. And that's when the real magic happens.

So, take a moment to ask yourself: *Are you willing to be that one person who thinks differently, who dares to step out of the matrix, and who is committed to creating your own path?*

If the answer is yes, then start illuminating your mindset today. The journey may not be easy, but it will be worth it. You have everything inside you to achieve greatness, and it starts with your mindset.

Once, Andrew Tate said something that struck me deeply: **"If God is going to give someone, a chance to become truly successful, He's going to make it difficult, He'll lay down a gauntlet, a challenge so intense that only the strongest will survive it. Why? Because within that gauntlet, some will quit, and those who quit, they become the losers, but the ones who don't quit—the ones who keep pushing forward, no matter how hard it gets—those are the winners."**

Think about it. Every time you face hardship, every time the road gets rough, that's God giving you another chance. It's not a sign that you should stop. It's an opportunity for you to prove something to yourself: that you will *never* quit. You'll stumble, you'll fall, you'll face moments of doubt—but you won't quit. And that's the moment that separates the winners from the rest.

The thing is, God doesn't just give you one chance to prove yourself. No. Over and over again, He'll put obstacles in your path, each one tougher than the last, to see if you can handle it. He's testing your resolve, your persistence, and your spirit. And those who continue, who keep moving forward despite every setback, they're the ones who win in the end.

The real key to success isn't talent. It's not intelligence or resources. It's the refusal to quit. If you can commit to never giving up—no matter how many times life knocks you down—you will eventually reach the point where success is no longer just a dream. It becomes your reality.

This is why the quote resonates so deeply: **"Tough times create tough men."** Every challenge you face is shaping you, molding you into someone who can withstand anything life throws your way. Embrace the grind. Keep moving forward, and remember: every difficult moment you conquer is one step closer to becoming the person you were always meant to be.

When life hands you countless challenges, it's not a sign of defeat; it's an invitation—a chance from God to overcome those obstacles and rise above them. In those moments, you face two choices: either you quit, surrendering to the difficulties, or you stand tall and confront them head-on, determined to reach your goal. The power to choose lies within you.

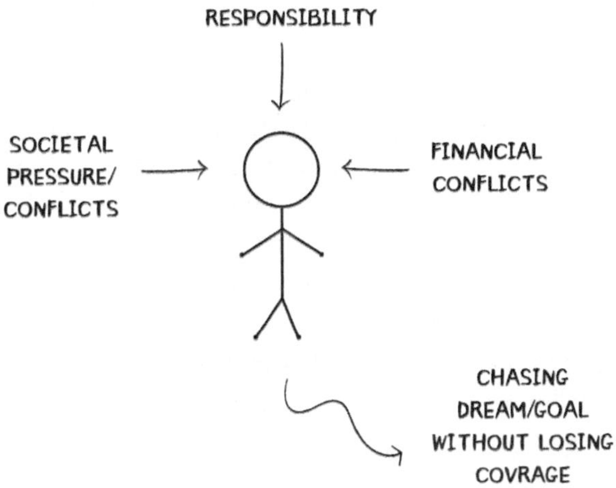

pressure

Every morning, when the sun rises, it serves as a reminder of the infinite possibilities that await you. It's as if the universe itself is encouraging you to paint the canvas of your life, but this time, with bold strokes of passion, purpose, and unwavering commitment. Your dreams aren't confined to what you can see; they are limited only by what you can imagine.

TRUST THE GOD

TRUST THE PROCESS

Everything begins with imagination. Don't limit yourself to small dreams—imagine big, dream beyond what you think is possible. But dreaming alone won't get you there. Break that big vision down into actionable, short-term plans. Take it step by step. Each action you take, no matter how small, brings you closer to your ultimate goal. That's the power of consistency and focus.

The true key to success lies in mindset. It's not just about imagining what could be; it's about believing in your vision and having the strength to implement it. The way you think, the way you approach challenges, that is what shapes your future. Your mindset is your most powerful asset.

As the great ones have said:
"Small minds discuss other people,
Good minds discuss events,
Great minds discuss ideas."

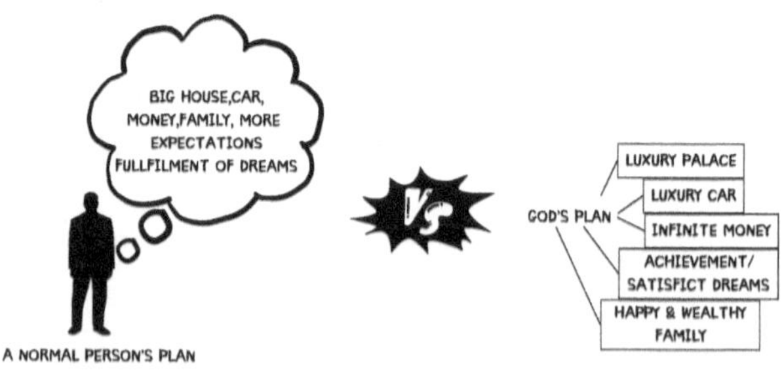

Greatness doesn't come from focusing on others; it comes from envisioning a better future, a better self, and a better world. The divine has a far grander plan for you than your own imagination could ever conceive. But here's the catch: you need to commit to it. God's plan for your life is bigger and better than any plan you could make on your own, but to unlock it, you must remain dedicated, consistent, and driven.

Donald Trump once said, **"In order to be successful, you have to find out what excites you. What makes you want to get up each morning and go to work? If you love what you do, and you dedicate yourself to it, then you will gain momentum. Each success will create another. When you do what you love, you can never fail."**

That's the essence of true success. Find what ignites your passion. Find that thing that drives you, that makes you eager to rise every single morning, ready to chase after your dreams. When you love what you do, the journey doesn't feel like work—it feels like purpose. And that purpose will guide you toward greater achievements, one victory at a time.

Remember, you have the power to choose. Every sunrise brings with it a new opportunity—a chance to overcome, to grow, to build. The question is: will you rise to meet it?

Weakness is a choice.
Winning is a mindset.

There's a powerful story about a small kid who once met a billionaire. The child looked up at him with sparkling eyes and said, *"One day, I'll be just like you."* Everyone around them laughed. It was almost comical to them—how could a kid, with so little, think so big? But the billionaire didn't laugh. He smiled because he saw something that no one else did. He saw the fire, the drive, and the most important thing of all: the mindset. He knew that kid would become a billionaire one day because the kid understood the power of belief, focus, and relentless ambition.

This brings us to an important question:

What exactly is mindset?

Mindset isn't just some buzzword—it's a way of life. It's the lens through which you see the world. It's the process of discipline, consistency, courage, and an unwavering dedication to your goals. It's about how you react when life gets tough, how you keep going when everything seems to fall apart, and how you rise after every setback. Mindset is the difference between those who give up and those who keep pushing forward, no matter what.

{CLEAR VISION + DISCIPLINE = GROWTH}

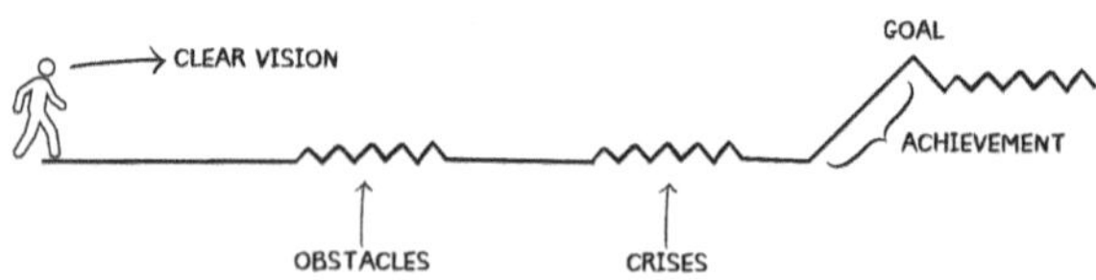

Think of a person's life like a stock market chart. There are times of rapid growth—those uptrends when everything feels right. But there are also those downtrends, when it feels like nothing is going your way. And then, there are periods of stagnation—the sideways moments.

Sideways is the toughest place to be.

It's the time when everything seems uncertain. The future feels foggy, and you're unsure about the next step. It's easy to get lost in this phase. It's easy to think, *"What should I do now?"* But the key in these moments isn't to rush. Instead, it's to pause, reflect, and observe. You need to wait for the right moment, to wait for the change in direction. The world around you will shift, and when it does, that's when you'll know the right step to take.

But here's the crucial part: **Never expect too much from anything or anyone**—especially from other people. Expectation is a silent killer. It can steal your power and destroy your ability to think clearly. When you expect too much, you set yourself up for disappointment, and that leads to confusion. The more you focus on what others are doing or not doing, the less you focus on your own growth.

Instead, focus on the present. **Be in the now.** The past is gone, and the future is uncertain. The only thing you truly have is the present moment. So stop worrying about what happened or what will happen. The more you get lost in those thoughts, the less power you have in the now—and the now is where all the change happens. It's where you build your future.

Today, people suffer because they're stuck between the past and the future. Their minds are constantly pulled in two directions, unable to focus on the most important thing: **the present moment.** The key to changing your life is realizing that the present is your starting point. It's where all real transformation begins

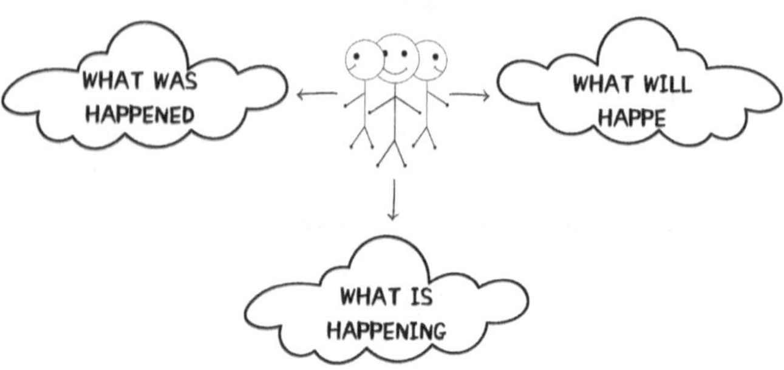

Take a look at the image above. It's not just an image; it represents a person with a different mindset. Just like a factory that turns raw materials into a finished product, a person with a strong mindset can take the raw material of their thoughts and actions and craft something extraordinary.

The same way that a factory operates within a particular timeframe—transforming raw materials into something valuable—*you too are constantly changing.* Your mindset, your personality, your behavior, and even your way of living are constantly evolving. With every experience, your thinking capacity expands. With every challenge, your resilience builds. And the more you dedicate yourself to improving, the more your mindset shifts, aligning you with your goals and dreams.

So, remember this: **The process of change is continuous.** Your mindset can either hold you back or propel you forward. It's in your hands. When you decide to commit, to embrace the present moment, and to shape your thinking, you become unstoppable.

∞

Key Points:

• 21 •

1. **Mindset shapes success** – Your thoughts and approach determine your outcome.
2. **Weakness is a choice** – Mental strength comes from resilience, not circumstances.
3. **Consistency is key** – Success is built through disciplined, consistent effort.
4. **Embrace sideways moments** – Pause, reflect, and prepare for the next step.
5. **Focus on the present** – Let go of the past and future to grow in the now.
6. **You are the creator** – Your mindset shapes who you become.

III

THE GREAT MINDSET AND GREAT TIME ALWAYS PAYS OFF.

How the Mindset of a Person Can Change Their Entire Perspective

Mindset is everything. It is the lens through which we view ourselves, our circumstances, and the world around us. The power of mindset lies in its ability to transform not just the way we think, but the very course of our lives. It is the driving force that propels us forward, even through the darkest moments, and the key that unlocks opportunities in times of struggle.

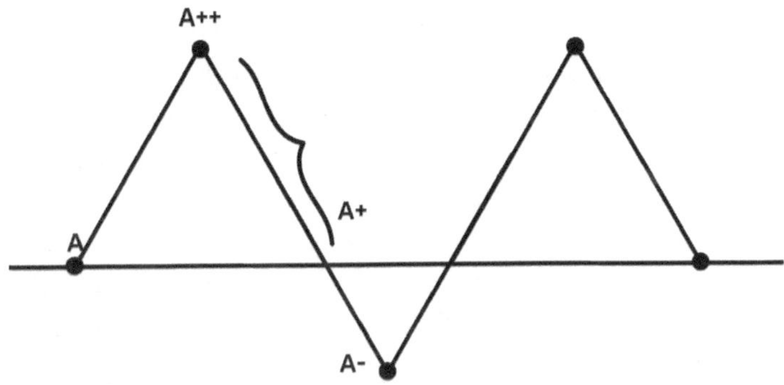

Let's take a look at the **fluctuating journey** of a person's life. Imagine it as a dynamic, ever-changing path—one filled with ups and downs, highs and lows. The way you respond to these shifts is what determines your growth.

The Phases of Life's Journey

- **Point A: The Starting Phase:** This is where it all begins. At Point A, a person invests time and energy into things that may not show immediate rewards. The path is long, the progress is slow, but they **believe in the process**. They are fully aware that the seeds they plant today will blossom into something greater tomorrow. The key here is patience, discipline, and faith in the vision.

- **Point A++: The Peak of Success:** At this point, the person begins to see the fruits of their labor. They are on top of their game—reaping the rewards of their consistency, hard work, and unwavering belief. This is the phase of **achievement** where dreams are realized. The person feels empowered, and everything seems to fall into place. But the journey doesn't stop here—this success is merely a checkpoint, not the final destination.

- **Point A+: The Recession Phase:** This is the phase where things begin to take a turn. The person faces a downturn—sometimes due to external circumstances, sometimes because of inner conflicts like **FOMO** (fear of missing out) or unchecked ego. They start to lose their grip on the behaviors and mindset that got them to the top in the first place. They may slip into bad habits or start comparing themselves to others, losing sight of their own path. The result? A slow descent.

- **Point A-: The Depression Phase:** This is the most challenging phase, the rock-bottom moment. At Point A-, the person feels like they have lost everything. **There's nothing left to lose.** But even in the darkest moments, there is one thing that can never be taken away: **hope.** Hope is the fuel that keeps the soul alive, that allows people to rise again. In this phase, they may feel defeated, but the process of transformation begins here. It's not the end; it's the beginning of a new chapter.

Life, with all its ups and downs, is an **infinite process.** There's no definite end to this cycle of growth and challenges. Every moment is an opportunity to **evolve,** to think differently, and to adapt your mindset to face the next challenge.

This cycle is constant, but the key lies in **how you respond** to each phase. Will you **stay stuck** in your setbacks, or will you rise stronger, wiser, and more determined? The answer depends entirely on the mindset you choose to adopt.

STRUGGLE IS PART OF LIFE

The Strength to Keep Going

It's easy to give up when life gets hard. **It's easy to quit** when things aren't going your way. But here's the truth: **It's much harder to keep going.** It's harder to stay disciplined, to keep showing up every single day, to put in the work without procrastinating, without excuses. The real challenge isn't in the work itself, but in pushing through the resistance within ourselves.

This world, as vast and unique as it is, was created by God with purpose and intention. Every part of creation is **perfectly designed**, each with its own set of challenges, skills, and solutions. Think about the creatures in nature. For example, sparrows build their nests using their innate skills, perfectly crafted to serve their needs. The nest they build cannot be replicated or recreated in the exact same way by anyone else. It's their unique creation—something that only they, with their specific talents, can make.

In the same way, you have your **own unique abilities** and skills. Your mindset, your aura, your way of thinking, and your approach to life are **incomparable** to anyone else's. **What makes you different is what makes you exceptional.** The challenges you face, the solutions you create, and the path you walk are all uniquely yours. This is what sets you apart from the crowd—this is your **power**.

Just like no two sparrows can build the same nest, no two people can create the same life. **Your journey is yours to craft**, and it is shaped by the choices you make, the mindset you adopt, and the perseverance you show.

The Infinite Process of Growth

There is no end to growth. You will continue to experience different situations with different mindsets and solutions. Life is a never-ending cycle of **evolution**—and each phase, whether of growth or struggle, is an opportunity for you to **transform** and become even stronger.

So, remember this: **It's not about avoiding the lows or fearing failure.** It's about embracing each moment as part of the infinite process of growth. With the right mindset, you can face anything, and with time, you will see that all the effort, struggles, and challenges **always pay off**.

Once Andrew Tate Said:

"Be a man, because a man is always faced with struggle while building his own world. A strong man knows that no matter what obstacles come his way, he stays focused on his goal. A true man has only one choice: 'Just do it.'"

Being a man isn't about strength in the traditional sense—it's about **mental fortitude**. It's about resilience in the face of adversity, the ability to keep moving forward when the world seems to be crumbling around you. **A strong man doesn't wait for the world to align in his favor; he aligns himself with his goals and moves forward with unwavering determination.**

It's not easy. Being a man, a person of strength, is **difficult**, and that's precisely why it's so powerful. It's about doing what needs to be done, no matter how much it hurts, no matter how many obstacles stand in your way. **"Just do it."** No excuses, no hesitation.

But there's more. In this journey, **faith** plays a crucial role. As the great ones have said:

"Pray like all depends on God, but act like all depends on you."

This is the powerful balance of life. **Faith** without action is meaningless, just as action without faith is directionless. Success comes from the fusion of both. Trust in God, but believe in your ability to take the necessary steps towards your dreams. Nothing happens without both.

The start is tough, but it gets easier.

The Struggle: The Test of Life

Struggle isn't something to avoid—it's something to embrace. It's a rite of passage. Every person on their journey must face it, and in doing so, they're being tested, molded, and shaped for greatness.

Struggle is not a punishment—it's a test. It's an examination in life, challenging you to prove that you have the strength, the courage, and the resilience to rise above whatever stands in your way. And this struggle doesn't just come once; it's part of your lifelong process. Each challenge, each hardship, is another test to see if you have the mettle to continue.

When the going gets tough, God may allow difficulties to enter your life, but it's not because He wants to break you—it's because He wants to see if you have the ability, the power, and the will to overcome. The goal isn't to remain comfortable; it's to become stronger through the struggle.

This is a reminder that every challenge you face is a stepping stone towards something greater. It's not there to harm you, but to help you grow. If you want to achieve something extraordinary, you must be willing to face extraordinary challenges. There's no growth without the grind.

Struggle: The Path to Greatness

Struggle is not just inevitable; it is essential. It is the only path that leads to something meaningful, something worth achieving. Whether you're facing emotional, financial, or physical challenges, the struggle is the crucible that refines your character. It builds mental toughness, it forges resilience, and it teaches you to never give up.

The truth is, struggle isn't just something you pass through—it's something that changes you. It transforms you. It's the test that prepares you for the rewards that await on the other side.

Remember this: You will gain something—whether it's strength, wisdom, or the success you desire—through the struggle. If you are willing to endure, if you are willing to push through, then you will win.

Facing the Critics

The journey won't be easy, and it will definitely not be quiet. Along the way, people will criticize you, judge you, and make assumptions about you. They will have opinions, no matter what you do. If you wear nice clothes, you're showing off. If you wear simple clothes, they'll think you're poor. If you speak your mind, they'll call you rude. If you stay quiet, they'll call you a coward. If you succeed, they'll say you're arrogant. If you struggle, they'll call you lazy.

The lesson here is clear: **No matter what you do, people will talk.** So why waste energy caring about their opinions? **Focus on your own journey.**

Don't let the noise of the world drown out your mission. The opinions of others are irrelevant to your success. Stay true to your path, no matter the judgments or obstacles you face. When you stay focused on your goals, when you embrace the struggle and keep moving forward, that's when you'll start to see the real progress.

Remember, **you are unique**, just as every person has their own path, their own skills, their own struggles. What you're going through is meant to shape you into someone who can handle whatever comes next. Your journey will not be the same as anyone else's—and that's what makes it powerful.

The Power of Persistence

In the end, it's persistence that wins. It's not about being the strongest, the smartest, or the most talented—it's about being the one who refuses to give up. Life will test you. It will challenge you. But if you continue to push through, to stay consistent, to embrace the struggle, you will inevitably emerge victorious.

Greatness is not born from comfort—it is forged through perseverance, struggle, and the unshakable belief that no matter how hard the path may be, you will not quit. Keep going. Keep fighting. Keep believing in yourself. The victory will come, and the struggle will have been worth every step.

Who Cares What People Think?

Sometimes, we spend so much of our lives trying to meet other people's expectations, but the truth is, **who cares what people think?** In the grand scheme of things, the only opinion that truly matters is **yours**. You are the one who has to live your life, make your decisions, and walk your path.

But here's a thought that might shift your perspective: Sometimes, God destroys your plans not because you failed, but because He sees that those plans would ultimately destroy you.

Think about it: God knows you better than anyone else—He knows what you're capable of, what you need to learn, and what challenges you must face to grow. Your life isn't just a series of random events; it's a divine script, written and directed by God. Every plot twist, every setback, every success—it's all part of the plan.

God has created this vast, beautiful world around us, full of creatures and elements that nourish the human soul. Nature isn't just there for us to enjoy—it's there to remind us of the power of simplicity and connection. The natural world has a profound impact on our mental wellbeing, emotional stability, and creativity.

Let's take a deeper dive into how the wonders of nature shape our minds and hearts:

1. Birds and Serenity: The Healing Sound of Nature

Have you ever stopped for a moment to listen to the birdsong in the morning? Birdsong has a magical ability to reduce stress and elevate our mental wellbeing. Studies show that the sounds of birds can help regulate our emotions, improve focus, and even make us feel more at peace with ourselves and the world around us.

When we pause and listen, we are reminded that the world keeps turning, regardless of our struggles. Watching birds flutter about brings a sense of calm, a reminder that life is as beautiful as we allow it to be. In nature, we reconnect with a rhythm that reminds us of life's simplicity and purity.

2. Forest Bathing and Mindfulness: The Power of Trees

Ever heard of forest bathing or Shinrin Yoku? It's a Japanese practice that involves spending time in forests and reconnecting with nature. Forest bathing has been shown to reduce anxiety, lower blood pressure, and boost mental wellbeing. Trees, with their vast roots and towering branches, have a calming presence that grounds us.

In a forest, you feel small and yet, connected to something far greater. The sights, sounds, and smells of the woods help us practice mindfulness, allowing us to be fully present in the moment. Trees don't rush, and neither should we. When we allow ourselves the luxury of stillness, we tap into a profound sense of peace.

3. *Butterflies and Flowers: Finding Beauty in the Smallest Things*

The delicate wings of a butterfly or the vibrant colors of blooming flowers might seem small, but their impact is immense. Watching a butterfly take flight, or a flower slowly bloom, can be a reminder of the beauty that exists in the simplest moments.

Nature's beauty is a balm for our weary souls. These small wonders have the ability to transport us to a place of awe and tranquility. In a world that's constantly on the move, stopping to appreciate these tiny miracles helps us reconnect with our sense of wonder and awe for life.

4. *Cats and Dogs: Companionship for the Soul*

Who doesn't feel an instant connection when they see a dog wagging its tail or a cat curling up on the couch? Domestic animals like cats and dogs provide us with unconditional love and companionship. They help us feel less lonely, less anxious, and more at peace with ourselves.

When you interact with your pet, your brain releases oxytocin, the "love hormone." This not only promotes happiness but also helps reduce stress levels, making your life feel calmer and more fulfilled. Animals have an innate ability to love us in a way that few humans can. Their loyalty and affection remind us that no matter how hard the world gets, we are never truly alone.

The Divine Plan: Embrace the Struggles

At times, God creates difficult situations in our lives because He knows that we are capable of overcoming them. He doesn't allow challenges to break us; He allows them to shape us into stronger, more resilient individuals.

When you face adversity, don't think of it as punishment. Think of it as an opportunity for growth. Every struggle is a test, a lesson that prepares you for the success that's waiting on the other side. **God believes in you—now it's time for you to believe in yourself.**

Andrew Tate's Wisdom: The Value of What You Have

Andrew Tate once said, **"If you know what you have, you don't have much."** This is a powerful reminder that true wealth is not measured by what you own, but by the strength of your character, your mindset, and your ability to persist in the face of challenges.

People often overlook the power of their mindset. The world can strip away possessions, titles, and material wealth, but it can never take away your determination, your resilience, or your will to succeed. Your mindset is what shapes your reality. It's the foundation upon which everything else is built.

The Power of Struggle and the Wisdom of Nature

God created the universe with balance. The struggles we face are a natural part of that balance—just as the peaceful moments of nature serve to remind us of our connection to the world around us.

In the end, it's all about finding balance. Embrace the challenges, the struggles, and the moments of peace. Trust the process and know that the difficulties you face today are the lessons that will prepare you for tomorrow. You are stronger than you realize, and with every setback, you are closer to the success you seek.

" The Story of mine"

It was back when I was in **10th grade**, just like any other student, hanging out with my friends, roaming around the school campus, lost in the world of teenage thoughts. We didn't really have a direction at that point—just a group of friends with no clear vision of what was ahead. But then, something changed.

One day, as we were chatting about random things, one of my friends brought up a name that none of us had heard before: **Andrew Tate**. He told us how Andrew Tate was this man who exuded a savage personality, someone who not only talked about changing your personality but also taught how to **break free** from societal norms, how to **become your best self**, and **how to win in life**. Intrigued, we all decided to check out some of his videos.

The first few videos hit us hard. They weren't just words—they were a wake-up call. We felt this surge of motivation, and suddenly we were all in the same boat, deciding that **we would start a business**.

But let's be honest—it wasn't anything unique. It was the typical teenage dream. We were just like every other group of students thinking we could conquer the world. You know the drill—those who sit on the last bench in class, joking around, thinking of "crazy ideas," but never really getting down to it. We were those guys.

There were two friends in the group—**Dev** and **Smith**—and together, we thought we could pull off anything. We did all the "crazy things" like making friends with teachers, trying to get good grades without actually putting in the effort. We became the "popular" guys, the ones everyone knew. Our bond, our friendship—it felt unbreakable. We created some of the best memories, moments that I'll never forget.

But as time passed, life changed. Reality set in. People drifted apart. My friends started focusing on their own goals. Some of us started following the norm, while others began to wake up.

You see, we were living in a bubble, blinded by the comfort of the school system, not realizing the truth that awaited us. And then, there were those two figures—Andrew Tate and Bruce Lee—who unknowingly played a pivotal role in our lives. They taught us things no one else dared to teach. They taught us to escape the matrix, to break free from the chains of mediocrity, and to conquer the present situation.

One thing they kept saying stuck with me: **"Remember, the truth is always bitter."**

That was it. The truth. We were not living in reality. We weren't embracing the real struggles, the real grind. And it's like they said: **"Focus on your goal, focus on yourself."** Because, in this world, **no one cares about you**, except for you. You are the only one who can take control of your life and shape your future.

The Truth About Life: No One Cares Except Your Parents

In this fake world, it's easy to get caught up in what others think of you, in the hustle of trying to be seen and appreciated. But the truth is, the only people who truly care about you—who genuinely want the best for you—are your parents. They are the real "hustlers." They sacrifice everything to make sure their children's lives are better than their own. They push through pain, struggles, and sacrifices just so their children have the chance to succeed.

I'm sure we've all heard the stories of mothers who carry their children in their wombs for nine long months, facing all kinds of difficulties to bring them into this world. A mother is a warrior, and her love for her child is unmatched. Fathers, too—they work tirelessly to ensure that their children never have to face the hardships they did. Parents are not just caretakers; they are the true heroes in the story of our lives.

And I learned this truth the hard way. Growing up in difficult circumstances, I saw my parents fight to make a life for me. And in those tough moments, my only goal became clear: **I will succeed in life, not for myself, but to make my parents proud.**

The Power of Struggle and the Ultimate Goal

This is where the real moral of my story lies: struggle. Struggling might feel like the hardest thing to do. It may feel like you're stuck in a never-ending cycle of failure, exhaustion, and frustration. But here's the thing—struggle is the only path that leads to something extraordinary. The struggles we face shape us, teach us, and ultimately, lead us to a future we could never have imagined.

Bruce Lee once said, "If you always put limits on what you can do, physical or anything else, it'll spread over into the rest of your life. There are no limits, there are only plateaus. Stay there, you must go beyond them."

This is the mindset that we all need. There is no limit to what we can achieve, except the ones we set for ourselves. The plateaus, the struggles, they're all part of the process. We must push beyond them, even when it seems impossible. That's when growth happens. That's when you start becoming the person you were always meant to be.

Struggle: The Only Process That Leads to Greatness

The truth is, success is not handed to you. It's earned through sweat, perseverance, and the willingness to face hardship head-on. And here's the thing: When you embrace the struggle, the universe will conspire in your favor. That's the power of a determined mind, of an unwavering spirit. You have everything you need to change your life—but you must be willing to struggle.

No one ever became great by avoiding difficulty. The world is full of people who shy away from challenges, who choose comfort over growth. But the true winners—the ones who rise to the top—are the ones who understand that struggle is the key.

This journey, this story, is about more than just a schoolboy dream of starting a business. It's about realizing that success doesn't come easy. It's about learning to focus on yourself, on your goals, and most importantly, on your own growth. It's about realizing that you are the hero of your own story and that the only limits you face are the ones you impose on yourself.

So, to anyone reading this, remember: embrace the struggle, chase your dreams relentlessly, and know that your journey is yours to own. Keep going, and the universe will find a way to make your path a reality.

A Man Must Constantly Exceed His Level

"A man must constantly exceed his level." This statement is not just a call to action; it is a philosophy of life. It's a challenge to go beyond the boundaries of who you are right now, to push past your comfort zone, to set higher goals, and to evolve continuously.

At its core, this idea is rooted in the principle of personal growth—the belief that growth doesn't have a finish line. It's an ongoing journey of improvement. Whether it's in knowledge, skills, achievements, or mindset, the goal is to constantly expand your limits and become more than you were yesterday.

Imagine this: you wake up every day and ask yourself, "How can I exceed what I did yesterday?" That's the mindset of a person who understands that true growth comes from challenging yourself—pushing beyond what you thought was possible. It's about creating a cycle of growth that never ends. This is how legends are made.

The Philosophy Behind Constant Growth

This idea of constantly exceeding your level resonates deeply in various areas of life, from ancient philosophy to modern self-help, psychology, sports, and more. Let's explore how idea plays a role in shaping our lives.

1. Philosophy: The Pursuit of Self-Overcoming

The concept of self-overcoming has been championed by some of the greatest minds in philosophy. Take Friedrich Nietzsche, for example. Nietzsche's idea of the Übermensch—the "overman" or "superman"—encourages individuals to transcend societal norms and surpass their personal limitations. To Nietzsche, self-overcoming is the highest form of life. He argued that a person must not be satisfied with their current state but always strive to exceed themselves, pushing beyond comfort and embracing challenges as opportunities for growth.

In other words, self-transcendence becomes the very essence of living. It's not about waiting for life to happen; it's about creating a life where you are constantly striving to be better—to become who you are meant to be.

2. Psychology: The Journey of Self-Actualization

Abraham Maslow's concept of self-actualization takes the idea of "exceeding your level" even further. In his famous hierarchy of needs, self-actualization is the pinnacle—the point at which an individual fully realizes their potential. But the key here is the pursuit of this potential. According to Maslow, once you meet basic needs, you're on a lifelong journey of personal growth, and there is always more to achieve. Self-actualization isn't a destination; it's an ongoing process of becoming the best version of yourself.

Maslow believed that we are all capable of achieving greater fulfillment as long as we continue to strive towards it. No matter where you are in life, there is always a higher level to reach. This is the essence of personal development: the idea that your potential is limitless, and that every step you take forward brings you closer to discovering who you are and what you're capable of.

3. Personal Development: Always Be Growing

In the modern world, the idea of constantly exceeding your level is at the heart of self-improvement. If you spend any time listening to motivational speakers, reading personal development books, or following high achievers, you'll quickly realize that this is the core principle they live by.

Leaders, entrepreneurs, and successful people from all walks of life talk about setting new goals and constantly challenging themselves to improve. Whether it's learning a new skill, developing a new habit, or conquering a fear, personal development is about never settling for what you've already achieved. It's about finding the next challenge, the next goal, the next level—and then going after it with everything you have.

When you make self-improvement your daily practice, you don't just live life. You master it. You rise above obstacles, push through failures, and refuse to let life's setbacks define you. Instead, you see them as stepping stones toward your next breakthrough.

4. Sports and Performance: Pushing Past Limits

Now, think about athletes—people whose entire lives are devoted to performance and exceeding their limits. From Olympic gold medalists to everyday gym-goers, athletes live by the idea that there is no finish line. Every time they break a personal record, they don't stop there. They aim higher. They keep pushing until they've reached the next level.

In sports, performance is not just about physical strength; it's about mental resilience. Athletes understand that the real challenge lies within—it's about controlling your mind, overcoming self-doubt, and getting up every day to do the hard work that others aren't willing to do.

Think of someone like Michael Jordan, who didn't settle for being good enough. He didn't rest on his laurels after winning championships. He was always looking for ways to improve, to evolve his game, and to reach new heights. For him, there was no finish line.

The Power of Tenacity

To constantly exceed your level, you need tenacity. Tenacity is the quality of unwavering persistence. It's the ability to keep going when things get tough, when failure knocks you down, and when others doubt you. A tenacious person doesn't give up. They don't quit when they're tired. They don't stop when the world tells them no. Instead, they push forward with relentless determination.

Think of tenacity as the fuel that keeps you moving forward when everything else is trying to hold you back. It's the difference between a winner and someone who gives up. It's about getting up one more time after each fall, learning from each mistake, and coming back stronger.

Tenacity doesn't just mean working hard. It means working smart, with a laser-sharp focus on your goals, and refusing to let anything or anyone derail you. It's about unshakable belief in your ability to grow, to evolve, and to reach the next level, no matter the circumstances.

Your Journey: The Endless Climb

The journey of exceeding your level is never-ending. There will always be new challenges, new goals, and new heights to climb. Success isn't a final destination; it's the constant push to become the best version of yourself. It's about looking at the person you are today and asking, **"What can I do better tomorrow?"**

Every step you take in this process of growth shapes you, molds you, and moves you closer to the person you were always meant to be. And remember, the journey of self-improvement is never about being perfect—it's about constantly striving for progress. No matter where you are now, there's always a higher level waiting for you. The question is: Will you reach it?

In the end, it's not the destination that matters; it's the journey. The striving, the growth, and the commitment to always exceeding your level is what brings fulfillment. So, don't stop. Keep going. And as you rise, remember: The best version of you is still ahead of you.

Here one is the most beautiful quote is,

"The heaviest things in this world is not IRON & GOLD, but the heaviest thing is the unmade decisions of the person, the reason is you are stressed is that you have decisions to make & you're not making them.

Once the great said that,

When the man blames other people than he has a long journey to cover, when the man blames himself then he is halfway there, but when a man blames nothing and just take the things as it is at that time he arrives.

Conclusion

In life, success doesn't just come from having great ideas or working tirelessly. It comes from two key forces: a strong mindset and the right timing. Together, these forces create an unstoppable momentum that propels you forward, even in the face of challenges and setbacks.

A great mindset is the foundation of everything. It's the belief that, no matter how difficult the circumstances, you can stay grounded, stay focused, and stay resilient. It's about understanding that every challenge is just a temporary roadblock—and with the right attitude, you can overcome anything. A strong mindset is what keeps you moving forward when the going gets tough, when things don't go as planned, or when failure seems to knock on your door.

But there's another crucial element to success: timing. You can have all the ambition and vision in the world, but without the right timing, your efforts may not lead to the results you desire. Timing isn't just about acting quickly; it's about recognizing the right moment, being prepared when that moment arrives, and knowing how to act when the opportunity presents itself.

The Magic of Patience and Preparation

Let's think about it for a moment: there are countless stories of people who have worked relentlessly for years, facing failure and delays, only to experience breakthrough success at the perfect moment. These individuals didn't let setbacks derail their journey. Instead, they kept improving, kept learning, and most importantly, they waited for the right moment.

Imagine someone who has been putting in the hours, working hard day after day, only to face challenge after challenge. But instead of giving up or losing faith, they build themselves up—mentally, emotionally, and physically. They keep going, not because things are easy, but because they trust that success isn't a straight path. They know that growth is a journey, and that with persistence, the right opportunity will come.

When the moment finally arrives, they are ready. They seize it. And in that moment, all the years of hard work, growth, and patience come together, creating a powerful alignment of preparedness and timing. That's when success happens—not because of luck or coincidence, but because they were ready when their time came.

This is the incredible combination of a resilient mindset and good timing. It proves that persistence, growth, and patience are some of the most powerful forces in the world. When you build yourself up, continue improving, and stay patient, you create the perfect foundation for success.

The True Rewards of Perseverance

So, what's the ultimate lesson here? Keep building yourself. Strengthen your mind, expand your knowledge, and keep growing—even when things seem difficult or slow. Success doesn't come from waiting for the perfect moment—it comes from preparing yourself for when that moment arrives.

Remember, greatness doesn't happen because of sheer hard work alone; it's the combination of timing and a prepared mindset that makes all the difference. Sometimes the most remarkable achievements occur when the right opportunity meets the person who has been working tirelessly to get ready for it.

Visualizing the Journey: A Metaphor for Growth

The image that represents this concept is powerful. Picture an hourglass on one side, with a small sapling growing at the base. The hourglass symbolizes time, and the sapling represents growth through patience. Over time, with the right nourishment, that sapling will grow into a strong, flourishing tree, just as your efforts and mindset grow over time.

On the other side, imagine a lightbulb or a brain with gears, representing your mindset—the ideas, the thoughts, and the persistence that keep you going. This symbolizes the strength and creativity needed to succeed.

In the background, there's a sunrise—a gentle and peaceful symbol of the reward that comes when you persist. The soft, golden light represents the moment when everything falls into place, when the opportunity you've been waiting for finally arrives, and your hard work pays off.

The overall design should be minimalistic, focusing on the essence of patience, growth, and mindset. It's not about complexity; it's about clarity, about understanding that true success is built slowly and steadily, through consistent effort and timing.

The Power of Timing and Mindset: A Final Reflection

In the end, remember this: Success is not just about doing the work—it's about doing the right work at the right time. Stay positive, stay prepared, and keep learning. When the right moment comes, you'll be ready to seize it.

It's about being persistent, being resilient, and trusting that with patience, everything will fall into place. The best moments in life come not just through hard work, but through the perfect intersection of a prepared mind and the right timing.

So keep building yourself, keep growing, and be ready. Great things are ahead, and when they come, you'll be the one who is ready to make the most of them.

Key Points:

1. **Mindset is Key**: A strong mindset keeps you grounded, focused, and resilient, even during challenges.
2. **Timing Matters**: Success is not just about hard work; it's about being ready when the right opportunity arrives.
3. **Patience Pays Off**: Growth takes time—be patient and trust the process.
4. **Resilience is Power**: Keep improving and learning; persistence leads to success.
5. **Success = Preparation + Opportunity**: Be ready when your moment comes.

IV

Worrier vs warrior mentality

*Life isn't just about fighting external battles—sometimes the real struggle happens within. The difference between a **warrior** and a **worrier** lies not just in how they face the world but in how they face themselves. It's about mindset, resilience, and the ability to either embrace challenges with courage or be overwhelmed by them.*

What's the Difference?

- **Worrier**: A worrier is someone who constantly feels anxious or stressed. They tend to focus on potential problems, often imagining worst-case scenarios. Their thoughts revolve around "What if this happens?" or "What if that goes wrong?" The worrier's mind can get stuck in cycles of doubt and fear, making every obstacle seem insurmountable.

- **Warrior**: A warrior, on the other hand, is a person who remains strong and resilient in the face of adversity. Whether they're in battle or dealing with life's challenges, warriors face obstacles with courage, persistence, and the belief that they can overcome anything. A warrior doesn't just fight external battles—they fight their inner fears and doubts, knowing that growth happens in the face of hardship.

Warriors: Real or Figurative?

1. **Literal Warriors**: These are the brave men and women who fought in ancient times, like knights, soldiers, or warriors of the battlefield. Their strength, skill, and honor defined them. They trained relentlessly to protect their clans or nations, often facing danger and even death without hesitation.

2. **Figurative Warriors**: These are the people who fight unseen battles every day. Whether it's a businessperson facing financial collapse, an entrepreneur overcoming setbacks, or someone battling personal demons, figurative warriors are resilient in spirit. They push through every failure, every challenge, and eventually emerge victorious. **Resilience** is their weapon.

3. **Modern-Day Warriors**: Take the example of a cancer survivor, a true modern-day warrior. Enduring painful treatments, fighting against illness, and facing the

emotional toll of such a battle—all with a positive attitude and unwavering strength. Their fight is not in the field, but in the heart, mind, and body. These warriors redefine courage.

Worriers: The Struggles Within

While warriors rise above, worriers are often consumed by self-doubt and anxiety. They constantly live in fear of what might happen instead of focusing on what *is* happening. Here are two common forms of worrying:

1. **Constant Worry**: This type of worry takes over a person's life. It's an incessant cycle of fear, usually about things that haven't even happened. The worrier finds it hard to sleep, often spending hours imagining worst-case scenarios. Whether it's about a career change, personal relationships, or just everyday decisions, the mind races with "What ifs?"
2. **Everyday Anxiety**: This is more common and less intense, but still pervasive. Everyday anxiety is the type of worry that comes from specific situations—social interactions, deadlines, financial stress, etc. It's temporary and typically fades once the situation passes. But in the moment, it can still feel overwhelming.

Say for example:

- social situations
- work or school deadlines

- money concerns.

Mahabharata: The Warrior vs. Worrier Battle

The **Mahabharata**, one of the greatest epics of all time, gives us perfect examples of how warriors and worriers exist even in the most heroic figures.

- **Arjun** – The Warrior in Crisis: Arjun, one of the greatest archers and a true warrior, stands out as an example of how even the strongest warriors can experience inner turmoil. At the beginning of the Kurukshetra war, Arjun is faced with a moral dilemma: fighting his own family, teachers, and friends. In the face of such a difficult choice, Arjun begins to feel overwhelmed by fear, anxiety, and doubt. He wonders if it's worth it to fight for a cause that requires him to harm those he loves.

His transformation from a worrier back to a warrior happens when he seeks guidance from Lord Krishna, who reminds him of his duty and purpose. Arjun's story teaches us that even the mightiest warriors can doubt themselves, but the key is to find the strength to rise above it.

- **Karna** – The Warrior with Internal Conflict: Karna is another warrior from the Mahabharata who faces immense external and internal struggles. A warrior by nature, Karna is known for his strength, loyalty, and courage. He fights valiantly for his friend Duryodhan, despite all the injustice and rejection he faces. He rises above societal constraints and faces battle head-on.

However, Karna also experiences deep internal conflict. He is burdened with feelings of identity crisis and loyalty, especially when he learns that he is the son of Kunti and a Pandava. This revelation leads him to question his place in the world and his loyalties, causing him to experience moments of worry and doubt. Despite this inner turmoil, Karna remains steadfast, showcasing the struggle that every warrior faces when their internal battles clash with their external ones.

The Balance Between Warrior and Worrier

What these stories teach us is that even the strongest individuals experience moments of doubt. A warrior's path is not without moments of anxiety, confusion, or fear. The key difference is how they handle those feelings. A worrier lets those feelings control them, while a warrior acknowledges them but doesn't allow them to dictate their actions.

We all face our own "Mahabharata" every day. Whether it's a big decision or a small challenge, we are constantly at a crossroads between choosing to be a **warrior** or a **worrier**. It's not about being perfect—it's about recognizing your fears and doubts and choosing to act anyway.

Choosing Your Path

The next time you face a challenge, ask yourself: **Am I going to be a worrier or a warrior?** Will I allow fear and doubt to stop me, or will I rise above them and fight? The answer lies within you, and it's in every choice you make.

Warriors don't ignore their worries—they confront them head-on, using them as fuel to grow stronger.

Worriers stay stuck in their minds, paralyzed by what could happen. But the path of a warrior is about **action**, **courage**, and **resilience**. Embrace your inner warrior, and no challenge will be too great to overcome.

Here I am sharing my point of view about warrior or worrier.

In my view, a **warrior** is someone who deeply cares for their family and friends—those closest to them. A warrior is a person who works tirelessly, not just for their own success, but for the well-being of their loved ones. A man, in my opinion, has specific dreams—dreams of earning more, of achieving success, and of enjoying life with the people he holds dear.

A warrior is someone who is always ready to overcome the toughest of situations, no matter how challenging they may seem. It is their courage, determination, and resilience that push them forward, even when the road is difficult.

Let's consider a situation or journey to understand this better. Our elders often say that a child learns many valuable things in the mother's womb.

Take **Lord Krishna**, for example. According to Hindu mythology and various spiritual texts, it is believed that Lord Krishna acquired divine knowledge while still in his mother Devaki's womb. This belief reflects the idea that Krishna, even before his birth, was a divine incarnation, endowed with wisdom and insight beyond ordinary understanding.

- Krishna was fully aware of his mission to protect righteousness and liberate the earth from evil forces.

- He is often viewed as an avatar who comprehends the concept of *Maya*—the transient nature of the material world.
- Krishna's knowledge of **yoga** and **meditation** is sometimes said to have developed even while he was in the womb.

This example of Lord Krishna teaches us that profound wisdom can be acquired even before birth. It highlights the importance of preparing oneself for life's challenges, both externally and internally, from an early stage—much like a warrior who begins to learn and grow long before facing any battles.

Now lets see the communication with devki.

Now, let's look at the communication between Lord Krishna and his mother, Devaki. According to certain **Puranic texts**, it is mentioned that Krishna could communicate with his mother while still in her womb, comforting and reassuring her about the divine plan for his birth and the eventual defeat of her brother, Kansa.

This communication serves as an example of Krishna's unique consciousness, even in his prenatal form. It shows that Krishna was already aware of his purpose in the world before his birth. He was conscious of the divine mission he had to accomplish, even while still in his mother's womb.

This suggests that Lord Krishna may have already developed certain skills in the womb, and after his birth, he went on to influence the world through his cosmic play. This idea supports the notion that a child can absorb significant knowledge and wisdom even before birth. Once the child enters the world, they continue to learn and are shaped by external factors, whether they are positive or negative.

Now let's see about worrier,

A worrier is someone who constantly thinks about other people or situations that haven't actually happened. They often dwell on scenarios that may never come to pass, creating stress and anxiety over things beyond their control.

As Ronaldo once said, ***"The past is the past, the future is the future, and the present is the best gift. So, live in the present and enjoy the world."*** This powerful reminder urges us to focus on the present moment, as it's the only time we truly have.

There was a time when I, too, was a worrier. I constantly thought about the past—wondering why certain things happened to me, questioning why I seemed to be the only one facing such challenges. At times, I also found myself worrying about what would happen tomorrow, trying to predict the unpredictable. The future is uncertain, and no matter how hard we try, it can never truly be forecasted.

In the process of overthinking, I lost sight of the opportunities and happiness in the present moment. This constant worrying led to stress and depression, affecting my behavior and interactions with others.

Here lies the key difference between a warrior and a worrier. A warrior learns to control their fears and impulses, taking decisive action even in difficult times. On the other hand, a worrier struggles to manage their thoughts and emotions, often becoming overwhelmed by anxiety.

As a great figure once said, remember this truth: "A weak man creates tough times, tough times create tough men, and tough men conquer the world."

The Story of Our Life is Written & Directed by God.

All our victories are dedicated to God, and all our losses belong to us alone. Life's challenges, the hardships, the difficult times – they aren't without purpose. God creates tough situations for the strong, knowing that only they have the strength, wisdom, and resilience to overcome them.

But what if a worrier is also a warrior? What if someone who worries about others, someone who carries the weight of the world on their shoulders, is actually displaying a warrior's spirit? Let's take a moment to think about someone who embodies both – a worrier and a warrior – **our fathers.**

Why Is Our Father Called the Great Warrior?

A father is more than just a parent; he's a warrior, a silent fighter in the battle of life. Why? Because, time and time again, he sacrifices his own comfort, dreams, and desires to ensure the well-being and happiness of his family. The world often sees fathers as strict figures, burdened by responsibility, whose focus is always on work and providing for the family. Yes, it's true – fathers may seem like they are always worried, caught up in the hustle to give their family the best life possible. They might not show their feelings the way we expect them to, but their actions speak louder than words ever could.

Think about it – when a child is born, it is the father who, in that moment of pure vulnerability, carries the baby for the first time. While the mother is overwhelmed by the intensity of childbirth, often unconscious or in a state of deep fatigue, it is the father who holds the child. He is the first to embrace the new life, to step into a new role, and protect the fragile little one.

This moment speaks volumes about the true nature of fatherhood – it's not just about providing for the family or being a "breadwinner." It's about **sacrificing** something precious to ensure that their child has the best opportunities in life. Fathers often sacrifice their own dreams, their own passions, and sometimes even their own happiness, so their children can follow their dreams and build a brighter future.

A father's life is a series of silent battles fought daily. Whether it's the long hours at work, the emotional toll of making tough decisions, or the inner struggle to balance family and responsibilities, a father's warrior spirit never wavers. And yet, this warrior is also a worrier – constantly thinking about his family, his children, their future. He worries about what's to come, about providing, about protecting. These worries, however, don't weaken him; they make him stronger, more determined.

In his quiet, relentless efforts, a father proves that **being a worrier is not a weakness**. It's a testament to his love, to the fire in his soul to protect and ensure that his family thrives. A warrior does not fear battle; he embraces it. And so does a father – whether he's holding his child for the first time, working tirelessly, or making sacrifices to build a future for his loved ones. He is the ultimate warrior, ever ready to face the fight for the sake of those he loves.

Fathers, in all their silent strength and sacrifice, remind us that the greatest warriors are often the ones who never seek glory. Instead, they fight for the ones they love, and in that fight, they embody the true spirit of strength, resilience, and love.

So, the next time you think of a warrior, remember the man who works quietly, loves deeply, and sacrifices endlessly. **The father is not just a worrier; he is the true warrior.**

The image above shows the sun, which feels most at ease with his mother, as he spends most of his time with her. This is the reality most people see and follow, but what they fail to recognize is that the father is working tirelessly to provide for the family and fulfill their needs. Often, this is why children may feel disconnected or even resentful towards their fathers. But the truth is, **the father is the one who worries the most about his family's well-being**. This is why we call him a warrior.

A father, like a true warrior, does not openly express his emotions. He keeps his feelings to himself, always working silently in the background to ensure that his loved ones are cared for. He doesn't seek recognition for his sacrifices; instead, he continues his journey, driven by a deep love for his family.

Here's the important distinction we need to understand: **The warrior and the worrier are two completely different things**. One represents strength, courage, and resilience, while the other represents fear, doubt, and hesitation. The worrier constantly overthinks and worries about things that are unpredictable or beyond their control. This mindset can be harmful because it leads to missed opportunities, and it prevents growth. A worrier's attitude might allow them to miss one opportunity without feeling guilty, but in the long run, this complacency will hurt them.

On the other hand, the warrior is someone who is always ready to conquer challenges. They face adversity head-on and take decisive action. The warrior believes that there is no time for hesitation. The worrier, however, is afraid of losing, and this fear stops them from taking the necessary risks to succeed.

The most crucial thing to remember is that **life offers us one chance – this moment. Play it like you've never won before**. Life is not about avoiding failure, but about embracing the fight, learning from mistakes, and moving forward.

God always has the best plan for us. The key is to trust in God's guidance, believe in yourself, and work relentlessly towards your goals. God places challenges in our path not to defeat us, but to see if we have the strength to overcome them. If we succeed, the victory is His, and it is ours as well.

So, take a deep breath, believe in the journey, and remember: **this is your last chance to play.** Play with everything you have, because the warrior who never backs down is the one who ultimately triumphs.

Conclusion

To achieve success and fulfillment, it's essential to understand the power of mindset, the value of time, and the distinction between a "warrior" and a "worrier" mentality.

1. **Mindset:**
   Mindset is the lens through which we view the world, shaping our attitudes, actions, and ultimately our outcomes. A positive and growth-oriented mindset opens the door to resilience, creativity, and the ability to overcome challenges. Those with a strong mindset approach difficulties as opportunities to learn rather than setbacks.

2. **Time as a Valuable Asset:**
   Time is a resource we cannot regain once it's spent.

Treating time as a precious asset means prioritizing meaningful activities and focusing on tasks that align with our goals and values. Effective time management not only increases productivity but also ensures a balanced and purposeful life.

3. **Great Mindset + Right Timing:**
Success often results from a combination of a powerful mindset and seizing the right moment. When we cultivate patience and stay prepared, we're better equipped to recognize and act on opportunities as they arise. The synergy of a strong mindset and strategic timing can lead to transformative outcomes.

4. **Warrior vs. Worrier:**
A "worrier" constantly doubts, overthinks, and hesitates in the face of challenges, leading to missed opportunities and limited growth. In contrast, a "warrior" embraces challenges head-on with courage and conviction, remaining undeterred by obstacles. The warrior mindset transforms fear into action, empowering individuals to move forward even when the path is uncertain. Adopting a warrior mindset while valuing time and remaining prepared for the right opportunities can be a game changer.

By focusing on growth, embracing challenges, and acting with purpose, we unlock our true potential and set the stage for meaningful achievements.

Key Points:

1. Mindset: A positive, growth-oriented mindset helps us overcome challenges by viewing them as opportunities to learn.
2. Time: Time is invaluable—prioritize meaningful tasks and manage it wisely for a productive, balanced life.
3. Great Mindset + Right Timing: Success comes from a strong mindset and seizing the right moment with patience and preparation.
4. Warrior vs. Worrier: Worriers overthink and miss opportunities, while warriors face challenges head-on with courage, turning fear into action.

Embrace a strong mindset, manage your time well, and act with purpose to unlock your true potential.

Final Words On "your Mindset Is Your Asset"

As you reach the final page of *Your Mindset is Your Asset*, I hope the words within these pages have sparked a shift in your perspective, encouraging you to recognize and harness the incredible power of your mindset. This book is not just a guide; it's an invitation to embark on a lifelong journey of self-discovery, resilience, and growth.

Remember, cultivating a strong and positive mindset is not a one-time task—it's a continuous process that requires dedication, reflection, and action. Whenever doubt arises or you need a spark of encouragement, I hope you'll return to these pages to reignite your passion and purpose.

Keep moving forward—growth doesn't end here. Let these principles guide you as you face challenges, celebrate victories, and learn from each experience. Use this book as a compass, pointing you back to the strength and potential within you.

As a call to action, I challenge you to take what you've learned and apply it to every area of your life. Share these principles with others—whether they are family, friends, or colleagues. Spread the message that our mindset is truly our most valuable asset. Together, we can create a ripple effect that inspires others to discover their own inner strength.

Thank you for allowing me to be a part of your journey. The time, energy, and heart you've invested in this process are invaluable, and I am deeply grateful to share this moment with you. Always remember, the power to transform lies within you.

Stay strong, stay committed, and let your mindset be your greatest asset.

Thank You

A Note On The Author

Krunal Prajapati is a driven student of business administration at UKA Tarasadiya University, with an unwavering commitment to achieving his personal and professional goals. His passion for success transcends the classroom, as he works relentlessly to build a life of purpose, resilience, and achievement.

As the author of Your Mindset is Your Asset, Krunal offers an inspiring guide for individuals seeking to harness the power of their mindset. The book encourages readers to stay consistent and focused on their goals, unlocking the potential for growth and success in every aspect of their lives.

Krunal is deeply passionate about bodybuilding, viewing it not only as a physical pursuit but also as a powerful metaphor for life's challenges. Through discipline, dedication, and constant self-improvement, he aims to embody the qualities of perseverance and strength—both in the gym and in life.

Beyond fitness, Krunal has set his sights on an even greater goal: to become part of the top 1% of achievers in the world. He is committed to building an epic life, one that is driven by purpose, continuous growth, and the relentless pursuit of excellence.

Through his writing and personal journey, Krunal aspires to inspire others to push beyond their limits, embrace their potential, and make lasting, positive changes in their own lives.

A Note On The Co-author

Dhruvil Patel is an author driven by a deep passion for exploring innovative ideas and empowering others to embrace their full potential. His literary works focus on inspiring readers to think beyond conventional boundaries and explore profound concepts that challenge their perspectives on life.

His book, Rabbit Hole Effect: Net, delves into the intriguing concept of the matrix, offering a thought provoking exploration that raises awareness about the unseen influences shaping our reality. Through this work, Dhruvil invites readers to question, reflect, and uncover deeper truths about the world around them

Dhruvil is also the author of Beyond the Script, a story about breaking free from the constraints of a traditional 9-to-5 lifestyle. This book resonates with dreamers and doers who seek purpose, resilience, and fulfillment in their journey.

As a student at UKA Tarasadiya University, Dhruvil combines his academic foundation with a passion for entrepreneurial ventures. With experience as a founder and co-founder of Lumiyan, Dhruvil has honed his leadership skills and a visionary mindset.

Dhruvil is committed to inspiring others to overcome challenges, break through limitations, and embrace a life filled with growth, purpose, and positive change.

Reach Out

Thank you for taking the time to read *Your Mindset Is Your Asset*. I hope this book has inspired and empowered you on your journey. I would love to hear your thoughts, feedback, or any questions you may have.

You can reach out to directly at:
Email: **prajapatikrunal393@gmail.com**

Or connect with me on Instagram:
@krunal___89

If you enjoyed the book, I would greatly appreciate it if you could share your feedback by leaving a review on Amazon. Your thoughts mean the world to me and help others discover the book.

Warm regards,
Krunal Prajapati